The Little Book of Answers

(Facts and Solutions to Several of Our Top Problems)

(Edition 1)

Neil S. Shifrin, PhD

Contents

1   Introduction

Some of the more pressing issues facing the United States are healthcare, taxes, sustainable energy, and climate change. The US shares these problems with other countries; this book presents simplified explanations and solutions for the US version of them. They are offered as a framework so that experts can then fiddle with the details. If these plans were implemented, perhaps they could serve as an example to other countries, particularly for climate change.

The US spends 18% of its gross domestic product (GDP) on healthcare. That is an incredible number. At least we have great doctors, hospitals, and medical research for all that money. But for a typical healthcare recipient, paying for healthcare causes major pain. A central problem is medical insurance. It has destroyed supply competition, which raises costs. How many patients shop around for an MRI (magnetic resonance imaging), despite wildly varying prices? It has created its own administrative ecosystem, which also raises costs. Doctors and hospitals must have whole departments just to deal with insurance. It dulls our senses to prescription prices, which again raises costs – all we care about is whether a pill is covered, not really what it costs. And to some degree, it dictates our treatment (or lack thereof), which can result in worse care despite our great hospitals. The only competition in the US healthcare system is for the price of insurance, a competition that tends to drive down the quality of healthcare.

Universal medical care coverage is not socialized medicine. It is simply insurance coverage for everyone, who can then access a free market of providers. Neither is it a "public option" socialized medicine. It is simply a government-run insurance company offered among a competing market of numerous insurance companies. These concepts are at the core of a healthcare fix, and they have nothing to do with socialism.

Healthcare's status quo would be to leave people uninsured. When an uninsured person gets treatment for "free," do you really think no one is paying? Universal coverage would simply make payments explicit, and explicit payments are the first rung on the ladder to cost efficiency. Healthcare cost data reek of opacity and confusion, as revealed by the painful research done to complete the chapter on it in this book. If the data can be truly sorted out, the urgent question becomes what will universal health care coverage really cost? To answer that, it is important to distinguish between shifted costs and truly new costs. The chapter herein attempts to do that. The US is unique in its emphasis on paying for health insurance through employment, and that is an important element to understanding shifted versus new costs.

There are many facets to US tax problems. One is that we don't have enough money for our rate of spending – the US deficit is on fire. For now, no one is paying much attention because interest rates are so low, but if they rise (when they rise?), the interest will cause serious hardship. Related to this is the byzantine spending of government, which means the spending of our taxes. The complexity of our budget, the weight of pork, and deficit spending leaves us blind to any possibility of understanding where our tax money goes. Moreover, the complexity of the tax code, with its 75,000 pages, works against tax equity and the US ever optimizing its revenue. Although tax equity is not the only thing creating an increasing divide between rich and poor, it certainly contributes, because some taxation is regressive, and the rich are better at dodging taxes with all the people they pay to read all those pages to help them avoid paying taxes.

The solution is not simply to raise taxes, however. Excessively high corporate taxes would drive tax revenue away from the US in today's global economy. Excessively high individual taxes could unfairly hurt many working people who already are just barely getting by. Rich people are an easier solution, but how rich do you have to be before it doesn't hurt? Do the very rich (a poorly defined term, except at the extreme) have an obligation to give back to the society that provided the platform for their success? Should corporations have a nationalist obligation, as long as they are not taxed into insolvency? These are philosophical questions.

The solution is to be smarter about taxes and spending – align taxes better with spending and eliminate deficit spending. If deficit spending is eliminated, tax increases would directly track government spending increases. Higher spending would mean higher taxes. That would allow taxpayers to know when to demand explanations of spending increases. States can't deficit spend, why should the feds? (The theory is the feds can, so states don't have to.)

The final solution offered in this book is about energy. Energy and climate change are inexorably connected, so the concepts are discussed together. As it turns out, fixing our long-term energy problems will also fix some degree of our climate change problems. While it is recognized that reducing *US* greenhouse gas emissions will not solve the *global* climate change issue, there are still significant benefits to doing it. First, the US emits about 14% of worldwide greenhouse gas (China is at 26%), so solving our emissions issues will at least put a dent in the problem. More important, however, is that such US leadership could incentivize and be instructive to the rest of the world. There is no question this needs to be done, so the US playing chicken to see who jumps first doesn't help anyone, including us, in the long run.

A presumably controversial element to converting the US to sustainable energy offered herein is the use of nuclear power plants as part of the array that averts greenhouse gas, with solar and wind being the other primary components. Two aspects make nuclear options controversial – power plant risks and safe disposal of waste. Several new reactor designs, such as Generation IV, may mitigate the risk of operating accidents that we fear could kill a plant's neighbors and create radioactive desserts. Generation IV reactor design also creates less nuclear waste. Nuclear power should be considered with renewed interest and with risk-benefit analyses in the context of climate change for it and the alternatives.

Safe disposal at Yucca Mountain, Nevada has already been designed at considerable cost, but it was killed by NIMBY (not in my backyard) politics. So, with our heads in the sand, our 98 currently operating nuclear plants just keep their 91,000 tons of high-level radioactive waste in their backyards and we have an excuse, albeit flimsy, for not building any more plants. There is no question that nuclear power is a force to be reckoned with carefully, but nuclear power makes sense from a technical perspective. It is politics and misunderstanding that make it senseless.

These four issues are not our only problems, but solving them would go a long way to improving life in the US in the long run. A few other issues are discussed briefly at the conclusion of this book. They probably merit chapters of their own, but then this would not be a "little" book of answers.

2   Healthcare Costs

The literature is replete with healthcare cost information (e.g., CMS, 2020,[1] Schreck, 2020,[2] CMS, 2017[3]), but it is difficult to organize it in a meaningful way because some of the terms/data are vague and spending vs. funding sources are difficult to sort out. The best judgment of this is that in 2018, US healthcare cost about $3.7 trillion (slightly more than the entire 2019 federal tax revenue) with the following breakdown:

---

[1] Centers for Medicare & Medicaid Services (CMS.gov). 2020. "National HEalth Expenditure Data: Historical." Accessed October 27, 2020 at https://www.cms.gov/Research-Statistics-Data-and-Systems/Statistics-Trends-and-Reports/NationalHealthExpendData/NationalHealthAccountsHistorical.

[2] Schreck, RI, MD. 2020. "Overview of Health Care Financing." Merck Manual, Consumer Version. Accessed October 27, 2020 at https://www.merckmanuals.com/home/fundamentals/financial-issues-in-health-care/overview-of-health-care-financing#:~:text=Health%20care%20is%20paid%20for,out%2Dof%2Dpocket).

[3] Centers for Medicare & Medicaid Services (CMS.gov). 2017. "National Health Expenditures 2017 Highlights."Accessed October 27, 2020 at https://www.cms.gov/research-statistics-data-and-systems/statistics-trends-and-reports/nationalhealthexpenddata/downloads/highlights.pdf.

Table 1. Where the Spending Comes From ($billions)

Private Health Insurance Premiums	$	1,200
Medicare		741
Medicaid		600
Out of Pocket		400
Other Gov Programs (e.g., VA)		150
Private Dental Expenditures		140
Investment		160
Public Health Funding (various gov)		80
Workers Comp Premiums		260
TOTAL	$	3,731

Table 2. Where the Spending Goes ($billions)

Private insurance OH and profit	$	200
Paid to Hospitals		1,200
Paid to Physicians/Clinical		700
Pub Health and Gov Programs		250
Prescription Drugs		350
Investments		160
Gov Admin		50
Home/Facility Care		250
Other Personal Health Care		480
TOTAL	$	3,640

The two tables' totals are close enough to serve as a confident cross-check, but the small difference demonstrates the difficulty in reconciling the data, which vary by source.

In Table 1, "Private Health Insurance Premiums" include all premiums paid by employers, employees, and outside of employment. The "Medicare" value is different than that presented in Chapter 3 because it includes both government and recipient payments. The value given in Table 1 was presented in the federal Medicare Trust Fund Report for the year 2018 describing Medicare benefits, administrative costs, and funding sources.[4]

Medicare Part A benefits were $308 billion, Parts B, C, and D were $432 billion. Part A is paid for from payroll taxes while the others are paid for by premiums and general federal taxes. Overall, Medicare is paid 36% from payroll taxes, 43% from government "general funds," 15% from premiums, 6% from "other" (unclear what), including some trust fund investment income.

Medicare has two trust funds. The trust fund for Part A (hospital) makes up any difference between spending and payroll taxes, and is projected in the 2019 report for depletion in 2026.[5] At that point, coverage will decline to whatever payroll taxes can

---

[4] Boards of Trustees of the Federal Hospital Insurance and Federal Supplementary Medical Insurance Trust Funds. 2019. "Annual Report of the Boards of Trustees of the Federal Hospital Insurance and Federal Supplementary Medical Insurance Trust Funds." Washington, DC., April 22.
[5] Ibid.

afford or payroll taxes must go up. Parts B (physician) and D (drugs) are covered by a different trust fund that never runs out of money because, by law, it must be supplemented annually by "general funds" (all tax revenues), thus putting increasing pressure on tax revenues as healthcare costs increase.

The "Medicaid" value in Table 1 is also different from that in Chapter 3 because it includes both federal and state money. "Out of Pocket" in Table 1 includes copayments and uninsured payments. "Other Government Programs" includes medical expenses paying for things like Veteran's healthcare. "Private Dental Expenditures" are payments made by individuals beyond dental insurance. "Investment" includes noncommercial research, structures, and equipment. "Public Health Funding" includes things like matching funds to state children's health programs, the Federal Employees Health Benefits Program, and the Indian Health Service, among many others. "Workers Compensation Premiums" are paid by employers.

In Table 2, only the overhead and profit portion of private insurance is listed in the first line to avoid double counting because the rest of insurance money is paid into some of the other line items. The other line items should be obvious except for the last, which is a vague term but probably includes dental spending, and expenditures for medical services generally delivered by providers in non-traditional settings such as schools, community centers, and the workplace. It would also likely include services by ambulance providers, for residential mental health, and for substance abuse facilities.

It is also useful to know how the US population is covered for healthcare (millions):

Table 3. US Population Breakdown of Medical Coverage[6]

Employer-provided insurance	156
Individually-purchased insurance	21
Medicaid	65
Medicare	60
Other Public (e.g., VA)	5
Uninsured	<u>28</u>
TOTAL	335

where the Medicare population includes about 20 million people covered by Medicare Part C, which is private insurance ("Medicare Advantage") reimbursed by Medicare.

The 2019 US total population was 328 million, so Table 3 appears to be reasonably accurate. These three tables can serve as the basis for understanding the true cost of a proposed universal healthcare, but the numbers are not yet in a useful form because they

------

[6] The value given for Medicare is from the federal Medicare Trust Fund report covering 2018 (Ibid). It includes about 20 million people on Part C, also known as "Medicare Advantage." Part C constitutes numerous private health insurance plans where the private insurance companies are reimbursed by Medicare. Presumably, beneficiaries decline Part B in lieu of cheaper Part C premiums that the private insurers run mostly like HMOs to reduce costs and thus reduce overall Medicare costs.

are not yet conducive to distinguishing between shifted and new costs, as noted in Chapter 1.

Shifted Costs

The purpose of shifting the costs noted above is to enable calculation of a per-person unit cost of money *currently being spent* whether via Medicare, private insurance, or for the uninsured. This will be done by collapsing some costs/spending into fewer categories and distributing out of pocket expenses to them.

The real cost of private insurance and Medicare currently being spent out of various pockets (employers, employees, etc.) could be considered to be all premiums, including those for workers' comp, and out of pocket expenses for copays and reserves. Add to that costs that we wish healthcare coverage would pay, such as refused procedures, private dental expenses, and prescriptions. Allocate these other costs between private insurance and Medicare, while separating costs for uninsured and you will get a current unit cost shifted to just three categories: private insurance, Medicare, and uninsured. Assume state-funded Medicaid continues, as is, but put it under "Medicare" to represent government-funded healthcare coverage.

The first step for this cost shift is to distribute the "Out of Pocket" line item in Table 1 to these three categories. Medicare's out of pocket expenses include plan upgrades and copays (e.g., for prescriptions). Out of the $400 billion out of pocket value in Table 1, assume 15% of it ($60 billion) covers Medicare out of pocket costs, and add it to the

Medicare costs in Table 1 for a new total of $800 billion. The uninsured's part out of pocket would be $190 billion if 10% of all hospital, physician, and clinical expenses in Table 2 go to pay for the uninsured. If 10% of prescription drug spending also goes to the uninsured, the shifted total cost of the uninsured would be $225 billion (there are probably more costs hidden in private insurance). That makes the shifted total cost of private insurance $1,610 billion/yr – the balance of out of pocket plus private premiums plus workers' comp. This shifts costs to all 330 million people according to the first three lines in the table below, while leaving $530 billion yet to be allocated for Dental, Government Programs, and Investment, summarized below ($billions/yr):

Private Insurance (177 million people)	1,610
Medicare + Medicaid (125 million people)	1,400
Uninsured (28 million people)	225
Dental	140
Gov/Pub Programs (including 9 million veterans)	230
Investment	160
TOTAL	3,765

Where the number of people covered is from Table 3, the unit costs of the three categories in the top of the above table are (per person per year):

- Private insurance - $9,100

- Medicare + Medicaid - $11,200

- Uninsured - $8,030

As a check, the 2019 federal Medicare Trustee report for 2018 notes a $13,257/yr "average benefit per enrollee," 16% higher than noted above, but the number above also includes Medicaid, which most likely pays less benefits than Medicare. This is a reminder that the services provided for these three categories are not equal, so it is no surprise that their costs are not equal. For example, Medicare generally offers better coverage than does private insurance and the uninsured probably get fewer services that the other two.

As a rough estimate, averaging the three and rounding up, assume a universal healthcare coverage would cost $10,000/yr per person. If the Dental and Investment line items in the table above are allocated to this universal unit cost, the universal unit cost would become $11,000/yr per person. Multiplied by the US population, 330 million, that would total $3.6 trillion. In addition, Government Programs cost another $230 billion for a total healthcare cost of $3.83 trillion, with universal healthcare coverage and a continuation of all government programs, such as VA (Veterans Affairs) costs of $106 billion/yr.[7] That

---

[7] Wikipedia.com. 2020. "United States Department of Veterans Affairs." Accessed October 27, 2020 at

is quite close to current costs. Presumably the other costs listed in Table 2, such as prescriptions and home/facility care are subsumed under the universal coverage cost, but this needs to be tested.

This means that under universal coverage, costs would shift, e.g., employers and employees might pay to a different entity but at the same rate as current amounts. Payments would not increase substantially. However, that "different entity" implies a new bureaucracy and an upheaval in the private insurance industry, both of which imply additional costs. The alternative might be to offer a "public option," which would be a government-run insurance company offered under the name of "Medicare" as an alternative to, but not a replacement of, private insurance.

Public Option Insurance

If a public option could be devised as an expansion of Medicare, it might offer less disruption to the insurance marketplace and incentivize private insurance to improve its coverage, because Medicare currently offers superior coverage. Assume it costs $13,257/yr per person as noted above from the trustees' report. If it were used to cover the uninsured as a "public option," that would total $370 billion/yr. With no other changes, that would translate to universal coverage for the US population:

---

https://en.wikipedia.org/wiki/United_States_Department_of_Veteran s_Affairs. Page last edited March 29, 2021.

- 177 million under private insurance, funded as current (employer/employee plus 21 million individual policies)

- 88 million under Medicare

- 65 million under Medicaid

- 9 million under the VA program

However, coverage might shift to other variations of this. For example, those covered under Medicaid and the VA program might shift into the public option bringing the total under expanded Medicare to 162 million. At $13,257/yr per person, that would cost $2.1 trillion. In addition, some under private insurance might buy the public option if it offers better coverage. Although this is hard to predict, an illustrative example with a public option would be as follows: the insured population would be about half private and half public, with the public option covering the currently uninsured. That would cost $2.2 trillion for public insurance and $1.5 trillion for private insurance, plus the $124 billion for other government programs ($230 billion minus VA costs) for a total of $3.8 trillion.

Thus, universal healthcare would cost $100 billion, about 3% more than current costs. This small excess might be reduced or eliminated if:

- A younger demographic profile under expanded Medicare could reduce its unit cost.

- Negotiating prescription drug costs could drive down the current total.

- Putting real buying competition into hospital and procedure costs or somehow standardizing them could drive down costs.

- Paying for the uninsured explicitly rather than opaquely, as is the current case, could drive down costs.

A final consideration under a public option is how it is paid for and how much would be subsidized by the government. Although Medicare currently is not subsidized in theory (in reality it is because payroll taxes do not cover its total costs), Medicaid is subsidized and the uninsured are subsidized somehow through current sources. Can the latter two categories be paid for by Medicare by shifting current funding from the federal Medicaid program, state Medicaid programs, and whatever sources currently pay for the uninsured?

The analysis in this chapter demonstrates that universal healthcare is financially feasible, and in fact, may not cost more than US healthcare's current spending.

3   Taxes

It is hard to believe today that there was no federal income tax before 1913, when the 16th Amendment established Congress' right to impose it. Now, it has become an opaque monster equated to the same inevitability and dread as death. Even when tax laws are changed, few people really understand how the changes will affect them or how the money will be spent (or not spent). This confusion is aided by our elaborate tax code, which is a testament to poor and well-lobbied legislation. But the cherry on top of this ambiguity sundae is deficit spending. It allows Congress to get away with just about anything.

The Federal Budget Process

Most of the time, the US operates without a budget, which doesn't help our deficit. Congress has passed a real budget only four times in the past 40 years. Instead, the US government operates under Continuing Resolutions or Omnibus Bills, which are poor substitutes for a budget.

The way the US budget is supposed to work is through a back and forth between Congress and the President starting every February and ending every September. Departments and agencies submit their budget requests to the President, who submits a detailed budget to Congress by February 1. Congress then passes a Budget Resolution, which is not detailed and merely establishes spending limits for agencies, not for programs. Congress then divides the discretionary spending portion (i.e., not health,

Social Security, agriculture, transportation, debt service, etc., which is about 70% of the total budget) of the budget into 12 detailed Appropriations Bills, which go to their respective Appropriation Committees for approval:

<u>Agriculture, Rural Development, Food and Drug Administration, and Related Agencies</u> - USDA (except the Forest Service) and other agencies;

<u>Commerce, Justice, Science, and Related Agencies</u> - Department of Commerce, the Department of Justice, NASA, and other agencies;

<u>Defense</u> - military, the intelligence community, and other national defense related agencies;

<u>Energy and Water Development</u> - Department of Energy, the US Army Corps of Engineers, and other agencies;

<u>Financial Services and General Government</u> - Department of the Treasury, the Executive Office of the President, and other government functions;

<u>Homeland Security</u> - Department of Homeland Security;

<u>Interior, Environment, and Related Agencies</u> - Department of the Interior, the EPA (Environmental Protection Agency), the US Forest Service, and a number of independent agencies;

<u>Labor, Health and Human Services, Education, and Related Agencies</u> - Department of Education, the Department of Health and Human Services, the Department of Labor, and other agencies;

Legislative Branch - House of Representatives (the Senate Legislative Branch oversees funding for the US Senate), the US Capitol, the Library of Congress, and other legislative branch functions;

Military Construction, Veterans Affairs, and Related Agencies - military construction (including military housing), the Department of Veterans Affairs, and related agencies;

State, Foreign Operations, and Related Programs - US State Department, USAID (Agency for International Development), and related programs;

Transportation, Housing and Urban Development, and Related Agencies - Department of Transportation, HUD, and related agencies.

Each bill goes to the President for final approval, all or nothing, without the opportunity for any "line item vetoes." If all 12 bills are approved by the President by September 30, we have a budget. If not, Congress can pass an Omnibus Bill, combining any unapproved appropriations bills into a single bill, or a Continuing Resolution to allow continued spending at previously-approved levels for a set amount of time. When the Continuing Resolution period expires without being extended, the government must shut down. Supplemental Appropriations Bills are also possible to add money to any pot (e.g., for disaster relief, war, etc.). These ad hoc alternatives to a real budget open the door to irresponsible spending. And when all this adds up to more than the government receives in tax revenue, we have a deficit, paid for by bonds issued to cover the shortfall. Wouldn't it be more effective to manage with a real budget?

Besides being irresponsible, non-budget operations make it even harder to connect taxes with spending.

The first step to stop the insanity is to require a budget process that concludes with a real budget. The other step is to ensure taxes equal that budget and any supplemental changes. Budget exceedances would only be allowed via supplemental authorizations (Acts of Congress), which would then be directly passed on to taxpayers. Taxes would go up if spending went up, thus alerting taxpayers to spending increases. This would make Congress more accountable. In theory, everything would be more explicit, more defensible, and more efficient. There would be no deficit spending.

A Simpler Plan

Many economists argue that financial leveraging (i.e., a deficit) is good, especially when interest rates are so cheap, and thus deficit spending should be encouraged. No one, however, understands just how much deficit is healthy, particularly when the future of interest rates is so unpredictable. If some amount of debt is good, the US could still incur debt without deficit spending. US debt could be acquired, as it is in the municipal bond market, by funding "one-off" projects. For example, need to fix infrastructure? Issue bonds to fund it. That approach plus working down our current COVID-19-bogged debt will give us plenty of leveraging for quite some time. The US government should function just like a responsible household – don't buy more than you can afford, but you can borrow to fix the house.

So how would it work? Taxes would be based on the spending budget. Taxes are paid in April for the preceding year so tax rates would be established two Octobers before the tax is due. (The budget for Year 1 is set October 1 of Year "minus 1" and the taxes for Year 1 are paid in April of Year 2.) Tax rates, described below, would be established on the basis of the budgeted *spending*. Currently, taxes are based on percentages of *revenue*, not *spending*, which is why there is a deficit. Therefore, this is a big change and could result in some tax increases, particularly at the corporate level. This will be analyzed and optimized to some degree below and certainly more so by tax experts. Another change from the status quo in this proposal is to eliminate "loopholes."

The ideal simplification to taxes would be to have a flat tax. Such an approach is regressive, however, meaning it hurts poorer people more than richer. If everyone paid, for example, 10% of income for taxes, that would take a larger relative bite out of a $40,000 earner's budget, who is already scraping by to pay for housing, food, and other necessities, than of a $2 million earner, who can easily cover even an extravagant living "nut" after paying the 10% tax. Rather, the distribution of tax rates should be as progressive as possible, increasing with increasing ability to pay.

If taxes and other financial policies became fairer, such as having a reasonable minimum wage, it might be possible to eliminate some of the fuzzy tax/spending feedback caused by subsidies. For example, a breadwinner working full time at the federal minimum wage ($7.25/hr) leaves a family of four 40% below the poverty line ($26,000/yr) so they need federal subsidies (from taxes), such as food stamps, to survive. Is there a minimum wage that would prevent or minimize this "shadow" spending of our taxes? Recognize, however, that keeping the minimum wage low is essentially subsidizing businesses that would otherwise have a higher payroll cost and perhaps thus pay lower taxes. It is a tangled web but if we could make it simpler and more straightforward, not only might government spending be more efficient, but also poorer working people might be better served.

The other element of this proposed plan, eliminating loopholes, would have the advantage of "what you see is what you get," i.e., the tax schedule would be *really* what is paid and thus could become a reliable planning tool. The term "loophole" is somewhat unfair because it implies deceit, but many "loopholes" are perfectly legitimate adjustments to taxes. For example, the mortgage deduction might be called a loophole, but it is openly at the core of our home ownership economy. The solution to eliminating loopholes is to make a tax schedule so reasonable that no one misses the loopholes. Imagine the deluge of self interest groups released upon Congress if such a concept were actually proposed. But proposed it will be herein because the justification is that this new tax rate schedule can stand on its own without loopholes.

Recalling that this proposed simplified tax schedule balances the US budget by being based on *spending*, not *revenue*, and eliminates loopholes, regardless of being legitimate or twisted, the plan is as follows (supporting data are presented later in this chapter):

A Balanced Budget
Based On *Spending* (not Revenue)

Spending	$Trillion	
Total Spending	4.5	2019 Estimate
Less corporate taxes	0.3	Current 7% of revenue now applied to spending
Less payroll taxes	2.2	16.5% of estimated $13 trillion total US earned income
Less other revenues	0.3	Current 6% of revenue now applied to spending
= Individual Tax Burden	1.7	Including capital gains and dividends

Revenue

Tax Bracket	Income Bracket ($1000)	Avg Income $1000/year	Tax Rate	Avg Tax per Unit ($1000)	Million Units	$Trillion Revenue per Bracket
Poor	0 – 25	<25	0%	-	16	0
Low Income	20 – 45	30	6%	1,800	41	0.1
Middle Income	45 – 140	100	9%	9,000	81	0.7
Upper Middle Income	140 – 150	145	11%	15,950	3.5	0.1
High Income	150 – 200	175	13%	21,875	13	0.3
Top 1%	200 – 2,000	450	17%	76,500	1.3	0.1
Top 0.1%	2,000+	7300	30%	2,190,000	0.2	0.4
					Total	1.7
Corporate						0.3*
Payroll						2.2*
Other						0.3*
Total Revenue						4.5**

*As noted above

** Sum of all brackets and other taxes

In the table above, "individual" taxes are either individual or joint returns ("tax units"), estimated at a total of 140 million. Individual taxes in the table include capital gains and dividend taxes, meaning that earned income would be taxed at the same rate as unearned income. This is an example of eliminating a "loophole," which is currently perfectly legitimate, but unnecessary. If the experts believe it is indeed necessary to incentivize investment (this is debatable), however, different tax rates for the two types of income could be restored with a slightly more complex schedule than presented in the table above.

In this plan, corporate and other (e.g., estate) tax *rates* are kept the same as current but their actual taxes will rise due to the shift of the rate now applied to spending vs. government revenue. But why shouldn't corporate tax payments be higher when large companies are obviously making so much money that they can afford $100 million golden parachutes, have CEO-to-worker pay ratios of 100+, and when 91 of the Fortune 500 companies recently paid no taxes at all?

If a new *spending* basis for corporate taxes actually threatens their solvency (which would need to be proven), the rate could be lowered, but it would mean raising individual rates. Alternatively, it might be possible to lower the spending-based corporate rate if the elimination of loopholes resulted in higher total revenue from corporations. Those 91 Fortune 500 companies would start paying taxes, for example.

Distinguishing corporate "loopholes" from legitimate business expenses (e.g., capital investment) will be the challenge of this plan for the tax experts, however. If a single corporate rate is too regressive for small companies, perhaps the schedule above could be divided into different rates for large and small companies.

"Other revenues" in the table above include estate taxes. The shift from rates applied to spending rather than revenue will result in an increase in the amount of estate taxes paid. Economists argue both sides of the estate tax amount argument - it should be low because it represents double taxation, or it can be high so that the next generation is leaner and hungry to create new growth. Currently, estate taxes constitute 2% of total tax revenue. Admittedly, however, converting it to a spending basis presents a challenge of how to design a rate because the amount of estate principal bestowed each year is unknown until it happens.

If more money from spending cannot be taken from these two categories, the alternative is to beat it out of the working people if deficit spending is eliminated. The alternative is to allow deficit spending to continue, which simply kicks the can to our children.

Besides balancing the budget, the appeal of this proposed plan is its simplicity and the fact that for the bulk of working people (the first five categories in the table), their taxes will probably be lower than they are currently, even with the elimination of loopholes and with higher capital gains taxes.

Payroll taxes remain in the plan as is because conceptually, they make sense. Payroll taxes cover Medicare, Social Security, and unemployment insurance. They should be thought of as workers putting money aside out of their paycheck for their retirement and rainy days, assuming the government doesn't squander the money (there are legitimate concerns about that). The company-paid half of payroll tax should also remain because it is reasonable to have a "company match" for such pension-type costs.

To make the proposed plan progressive, the individual tax rate increases, with an increasing income bracket, from 0% to 30%. Note these are not marginal rates, they are overall rates. The rates should be viewed as reasonable for each income bracket because they probably result in lower taxes paid than under the current system. (This should be examined by the experts.)

Families ("tax units") earning below the poverty line should pay no tax because they will still need government subsidies to live. For a family/tax unit earning $150,000, their 11% tax rate ($16,500) should be reasonably manageable among their other living expenses. For a $2 million earner, a $600,000 tax (30%) still leaves a tidy sum ($1.4 million/yr) to live on while serving as a hefty funder (24% of the total) of government spending, in return for the government having provided the infrastructure that enabled the wealth in the first place. Libertarians might argue that such a bite in income will disincentivize entrepreneurship, but it is doubtful that this rate is onerous enough to discourage anyone determined to get rich.

It was said before, but it is worth saying again – these overall, not marginal rates, meaning "what you see is what you get," have the tremendous benefit of being a transparent planning tool.

The relative fractions of spending paid by different tax sources is also of interest for considering fairness. In the proposed plan, individual taxes pay for 38% of spending while corporate taxes pay only 7%. The tax experts should decide if this is fair. Payroll taxes pay for 49% of spending, which still doesn't totally cover Medicare, Social Security, and unemployment benefits.[8] Should they be better aligned? In the proposed plan, payroll taxes are 130% of the individual income tax contribution to government spending. In the end, non-discretionary spending must get paid one way or the other, so which tax vehicle is the most equitable?

If this plan could really work, perhaps we could pare down the tax code from 75,000 pages to 10 or 100 pages. That might make the 800,000 tax accountants in the US nervous about their $7.4 billion/yr revenue, however.

The Underlying Facts

The plan proposed above was devised based upon a number of facts about US spending and taxes. The information presented below serves as that basis and also contains some facts to provide perspective on taxes and government spending. Research has shown that the numbers below might vary slightly depending on the source of the information, but what is presented below is believed to be close to accurate. Experts might hone better accuracy, but it is unlikely to change the viability of the plan.

---

[8] DeSilver, D. 2017. "What does the federal government spend your tax dollars on? Social insurance programs, mostly." Pew Research Center. Accessed October 27, 2020 at https://www.pewresearch.org/fact-tank/2017/04/04/what-does-the-federal-government-spend-your-tax-dollars-on-social-insurance-programs-mostly/.

- In 2019, the US spent \$4.5 trillion.[9]

- 2019 US tax revenue was \$3.5 trillion[10] (thus, the deficit of about \$1 trillion, before the COVID-19 pandemic):

> - 7% of revenues were from corporate taxes
>
> - 49% from individual/joint taxes
>
> - 36% from "payroll taxes" that pay for Social Security, Medicare, and unemployment insurance
>
> - 8% from things like estate taxes (2%), excise tax, and tariffs (4%)

- 47% of federal spending is mandatory for health and retirement:[11]

> - 23% (of total spending) for Social Security (\$1 trillion)
>
> - 15% for Medicare (\$644 billion) and 9% for Medicaid (\$409 billion)

- 24% of federal spending is mandatory for other requirements:[12]

---

[9] Amadeo, K. 2021. "FY 2019 Federal Budget: Trump's Budget Request." Accessed October 27, 2020 at https://www.thebalance.com/fy-2019-federal-budget-summary-of-revenue-and-spending-4589082. Updated January 19.

[10] Congressional Budget Office. 2019. "Monthly Budget Review: Summary for Fiscal Year 2019." November 7. 5p. Accessed October 27, 2020 at https://www.cbo.gov/system/files/2019-11/55824-CBO-MBR-FY19.pdf.

[11] Congressional Budget Office. 2020. "The Federal Budget in 2019: An Infographic." April 15. Accessed October 27, 2020 at https://www.cbo.gov/publication/56324.

[12] Ibid.

- 15% for unemployment compensation, federal/military retirement, some veterans programs, and some poor assistance programs ($642 billion, total)

- 9% for debt interest ($375 billion)

- Conversely, from the above, US discretionary spending is only 29% of the total. This includes defense spending, which is about half ($680 billion).

- In 2019, payroll taxes totaled $1.2 trillion[13] (27% of spending). Employers and employees share this tax:[14] 6.2% of employee earnings each from employer and employee (capped at $133,000 of earnings) for Social Security, 1.45% of employee earnings each from employer and employee for Medicare, and 1.2% of employee earnings from employer for unemployment.

- In 2017, 143 million taxpayers ("taxpayer units") earned $11 trillion and paid $1.6 trillion in individual/joint income

---

[13] Ibid.

[14] Blakely-Gray, R. 2020. What Are the Payroll Taxes Paid by Employer?" February 19. Accessed October 27, 2020 at https://www.patriotsoftware.com/blog/payroll/payroll-taxes-paid-by-employer/#:~:text=So%2C%20what%20percentage%20of%20payroll,the%20Social%20Security%20wage%20base.

taxes.[15] (Other estimates go as high as $13 trillion/yr.) Presumably, the difference between that number and 49% of $3.5 trillion ($1.72 trillion) is capital gains and dividend tax.

- At $11 trillion of total income, the average income of a taxpayer unit was $77,000/yr ($11 trillion divided by 143 million units).

- From another reference, the average family income is $76,000/yr (2014);[16] the median is $69,000 (2019).[17]

- In 2017, the top 50 percent of all taxpayers paid 97 percent of all individual income taxes while the bottom 50 percent paid the remaining 3 percent.[18]

---

[15] York, E. 2020. February 25. "Summary of the Latest Federal Income Tax Data, 2020 Update." Accessed October 27, 2020 at https://taxfoundation.org/summary-of-the-latest-federal-income-tax-data-2020-update/.

[16] Wikipedia.com. 2020. "Household Income in the United States." Accessed October 27, 2020 at https://en.wikipedia.org/wiki/Household_income_in_the_United_States. Page last updated April 12, 2021.

[17] Semega, J; Kollar, M; Shrider, EA; & Creamer, J. 2020. Income and Poverty in the United States: 2019. September 15. Accessed October 27, 2020 at https://www.census.gov/library/publications/2020/demo/p60-270.html#:~:text=Median%20household%20income%20was%20%2468%2C703,and%20Table%20A%2D1).

[18] Bellafiore, R. 2018. "Summary of the Latest Federal Income Tax Data, 2018 Update." November 13. Accessed October 27, 2020 at https://taxfoundation.org/summary-latest-federal-income-tax-data-2018-update/#:~:text=The%20top%201%20percent%20of%20taxpayers%20paid%20roughly%20%24538%20billion,percent%20of%20all%20income%20taxes.

- The top 1 percent of earners (>$420,000/yr) paid 37% of individual income taxes.[19]

- Although there are many versions of this, one source said:[20]

Household Income Range	Number of Households (Millions)	% of Total	Category
Less than $20,000	16.8	13.1%	Below or near poverty level
$20,000 - $44,999	25.8	20%	Low income
$45,000 - $139,999	59.3	46.1%	Middle class
$140,000 - $149,999	2.7	2.1%	Upper middle class
$150,000 - $199,999	10.6	8.2%	High income
$200,000+	13.2	10.3%	Highest tax brackets

- The federal poverty limit for a family of four is about $26,000/yr.[21] Households making less than this are eligible for subsidies such as food stamps and an earned income tax credit.

---

[19] Ibid.

[20] Amadeo, K & Howard, EJ. 2020. "What Is Middle-Class Income?" October 24. Accessed October 27, 2020 at https://www.thebalance.com/definition-of-middle-class-income-4126870.

[21] Paying for Senior Care. 2020. "2020 Health & Human Services Poverty Guidelines / Federal Poverty Levels." August 23. Accessed October 27, 2020 at https://www.payingforseniorcare.com/federal-poverty-level.

- An estimated 38 million people live below the poverty line.[22] This is 12% of the US population and these people may not even be counted among the 140 million taxpayer units.

Two of the more surprising facts from above are the amount of mandatory budget (about 70%) and the relatively small contribution of corporate tax to the government budget (7%).

The proposed plan in this chapter shows that deficit spending can be eliminated, and a more transparent tax schedule can be devised that most likely lowers most taxpayers´ burden, even without loopholes and a lower capital gains rate. More thought may be merited on a corporate tax schedule that is fair and balanced relative to the household/individual/worker tax burden, but this is not expected to disqualify the proposed plan.

----

[22] Fessler, P. 2019. "U.S. Census Bureau Reports Poverty Rate Down, But Millions Still Poor." NPR.org. September 10. Accessed October 27, 2020 at https://www.npr.org/2019/09/10/759512938/u-s-census-bureau-reports-poverty-rate-down-but-millions-still-poor#:~:text=Despite%20the%20decline%20in%20poverty,two%20adults%20and%20two%20children.

4   Sustainable Energy

Two forces drive a need to transition off fossil fuels – climate change and depletable resources. Deniers and politicians (often the same thing) want to kick the can down the road, either to avoid being blamed for the pain of transition or in the hope that a silver bullet will be discovered in the future. Conversely, they just can't read the writing on the wall. More than 99% of scientists do not deny climate change.

Like it or not, the plan described below is where we must be someday. We have a choice for how to embrace it – determined leadership for an organized transition, or haphazard foot dragging with incremental changes while mopping up the problems that delay will cause. Delay undoubtedly will make a transition more expensive (e.g., building higher seawalls) and more painful. Worse, it might ruin everything. We should get started today.

So, what's it going to take to make energy sustainable and to save the planet? Basically, we must replace fossil fuels and sequester as much atmospheric carbon as possible. The key is generally to convert everything to electricity, since electricity can be generated without fossil fuels while being transmissible and storable. The plan is described below, but first is a reference table of 2019 US energy use that can be derived from the underlying factual information presented later in this chapter.

	Current Direct Fossil Energy*	Plus Current Electricity Use*
Transportation	28	Negligible
Industrial	26.4	6.6
Commercial	4.7	13.3
Residential	7	14

Quadrillion BTU/yr (Quads or Q) – 2019 US Total = 100 Q

The plan would be:

Electricity (34Q) – replace all fossil generation with a combination of solar, wind, and nuclear. This will require 7 trillion *new* Kwhr/yr (including accounting for system losses of about 3% and in addition to the current renewable fraction) in the form of centralized sources (e.g., power plants converted to wind, solar, and nuclear) and additional distributed sources (e.g., rooftop solar cells), averting 1.5 billion tons/yr of greenhouse gas (in 2019, the US emitted 6.7 billion tons/yr, China emitted 14).

Transportation (28Q) – replace all land transport fossil with electric, equivalent to 6 trillion Kwhr/yr of new, non-fossil electric generation, averting 1.3 billion tons/yr of greenhouse gas. Tolerate, until there is a technical solution, fossil-fueled air and marine transport, equivalent to 1.4 billion barrels of oil/yr (the US currently uses 18 billion barrels/yr), which will continue to emit 0.5 billion tons/yr of greenhouse gas. But this continuing emitted carbon will be offset with atmospheric sequestration.

Industrial (33Q) – Most industrial energy is used to generate what is called "process heat" (e.g., boilers, melting, etc.), leaving only about 5% for space heating. Some process heat is already generated from electricity (e.g., aluminum smelting), so assume 20% of total industrial energy is already from electricity, which was already converted to non-fossil as described above. By 2040, retrofit half of the remaining 80% of now fossil energy to electricity or to onsite renewables, leaving 40% of industrial energy as fossil with its greenhouse gas sequestered after 2040. (Hopefully, we could do better than this.)

Commercial (18Q) – 25% of commercial energy is for space heating. Assume half of that is electric HVAC, leaving commercial's fossil use as 12.5% of its total energy use. The remaining 87.5% is already electric, which was converted to non-fossil as described above. By 2040, convert half of the commercial fossil heating to non-fossil leaving the rest as fossil with greenhouse gas sequestration.

Residential (21Q) – 43% of residential energy is for space heating. Assume 35% is fossil-fueled with the balance (e.g., air conditioning, lighting, etc.) using electricity. That means residential energy is 65% electricity, which was already converted to non-fossil as described above. By 2040, convert half of residential fossil heating to non-fossil, leaving the rest as fossil with greenhouse gas sequestration.

("Industry" is things like factories, while "commercial" is things like office buildings and malls.)

This plan requires about 18.4 trillion Kwhr of new, renewable electricity and, by 2040, averts 4.4 billion tons/yr of greenhouse gas. After 2040, about 2.3 billion tons/yr of greenhouse gas will still be emitted until we can figure out how to wean the rest off fossil fuels (1.9 billion tons/yr) and to fix agriculture (0.4 billion tons/yr). Thus, by 2040, the plan would eliminate all but about 4 billion barrels of oil burned per year and reduce greenhouse gas emissions by 60%. A table summarizing this plan is presented at the end of this chapter. A very simplified estimate of what the plan would cost is:

New electricity – $11.6 trillion capital cost (about half of US GDP), based on a recently installed Japanese large solar array described below, assuming 1 Kw of installed renewable capacity will generate 1,000 Kwh/yr.

Carbon sequestration – $230 billion/yr, based on an optimistic cost estimate of $100/ton to address the 2.3 billion tons/yr remaining after 2040. This is about a third of the US defense budget. More could be spent if we also deal with the ramp-down period. Note that "sequestration" is still a vague term due to the current nascence of its technology.

The technologies for electric generation conversion are available today. Carbon sequestration technology still has development challenges, but from current descriptions in the literature, they don't appear to be insurmountable. Retrofitting space heating and some of industrial process heat will require some innovation or clever adaptation of existing technology. Conversion of the entire land transportation fleet to electricity will require storage battery improvements and a new infrastructure for "fueling." More nuclear for the electric conversion is advisable, but fuel waste storage is an issue to be resolved. The US has already spent billions studying Yucca Mountain (Nevada) for permanent storage of the nation's high-level radioactive waste, which is an excellent site (e.g., geologically stable) with transport designed to withstand a locomotive crash, but NIMBY politics killed it. It should be reconsidered.

Further thought will likely offer tweaks to the plan, reconciliation of the source-varying factual data, and to the table at the end. For example, the table lists zeros for current non-fossil energy use in several sectors, but that is not exactly true. These adjustments are likely to be relatively minor, however, and are not expected to change the overall approach or feasibility of the presented plan.

Economists should have a ball with these numbers. First, they mix capital and operating costs, and it is not simple to separate the two. Solar electricity should be low on operating costs, but far from zero and the numbers above don't include them. Carbon sequestration operating costs discussed in literature describing pilot plants must already have capital amortization built in, given the way costs of the technology are described. In addition, more new electricity will be required to operate sequestration. Furthermore, the costs presented above are not unique, meaning that some of this money would be spent anyway on fossil technology.

For example, replacement costs for current fossil technology could be applied to some of the renewables' conversion cost. The time value of money needs considering for this 20-year transition and for renewables operating costs. Optimization also needs considering. For example, the simplified cost estimate simply scaled up one solar example in Japan for electricity conversion, but in reality, the conversion will consist of some optimized combination of wind, nuclear, solar, and centralized/distributed systems.

In addition, there will be many costs of associated adaptation technology. For example, all those electric vehicles need to be developed/manufactured along with better storage technology, not to mention the technical challenges remaining for carbon sequestration. There are also issues of how to pay for this. For example, carbon sequestration can be paid for by a carbon tax, but such a tax will likely be passed on to consumers. There are also pragmatic issues like where to put all those solar cells.

Undoubtedly, many more economic and technology, not to mention societal and even political considerations, exist. The important issue, however, is that these numbers, although they might be painful, are not prohibitive. The technology is feasible and to a large degree already available. There is no need to wait for a silver bullet that is unlikely to materialize.

The 20-year transition period is also feasible, and it is convenient, considering that much of the fossil technology to be replaced will be due for rebuilding during that period anyway.

There is no question that spending half of GDP on a new infrastructure and about a quarter of the defense budget equivalent for ongoing sequestration will be disruptive. But will it be more disruptive than climate change?

The facts underlying the plan numbers presented above are recent US figures unless noted otherwise. All web references were accessed on October 27, 2020; many numbers are rounded:

- The US uses 100 quadrillion BTUs/yr (Quads).[23] This is equivalent to 18 billion barrels of oil[24] (49 million barrels a day). The US consumes 17% of the world's energy.[25]

> - 1 Quad = 300 billion Kwhr = 180 million barrels of oil = 39 million tons of coal = 1 trillion cu ft of gas (approximately)[25]

---

[23] U.S. Energy Information Administration (EIA). 2020a. "Frequently Asked Questions (FAQs): What is the United States' share of world energy consumption?" Accessed October 27, 2020 at https://www.eia.gov/tools/faqs/faq.php?id=87&t=1#:~:text=What%20is%20the%20United%20States,of%20about%20582%20quadrillion%20Btu. Page last updated December 15, 2020.

[24] Britannica.com. 2020. "Quad, measurement." Accessed October 27, 2020 at https://www.britannica.com/science/quad.

[25] U.S. Energy Information Administration (EIA). 2020a. "Frequently Asked Questions (FAQs): What is the United States' share of world energy consumption?" Accessed October 27, 2020 at https://www.eia.gov/tools/faqs/faq.php?id=87&t=1#:~:text=What%20is%20the%20United%20States,of%20about%20582%20quadrillion%20Btu. Page last updated December 15, 2020.

- Energy is supplied by the following primary fuels: 37% petroleum, 32% natural gas, 11% coal, 8% nuclear, and 11% renewables.[26]

> - The renewables breakdown is about 27% wind, 25% hydro, 23% biofuels, 20% wood, 10% solar, 4% waste, and 2% geothermal.[27]

> - The US uses 140 billion gallons/yr of gasoline.[28]

> - 37% of US energy is in the form of electricity.[29] Nearly all of this is sold to four sectors, described below.

- Primary fuel use by sector is: 28% transportation, 23% industry, 7% residential, and 5% commercial.[30]

---

[26] U.S. Energy Information Administration (EIA). 2020b. "U.S. energy facts explained." Accessed October 27, 2020 at https://www.eia.gov/energyexplained/us-energy-facts/.

[27] Center for Sustainable Systems, University of Michigan. 2020a. "U.S. Renewable Energy Factsheet." Pub. No. CSS03-12. Accessed October 27, 2020 at http://css.umich.edu/factsheets/us-renewable-energy-factsheet.

[28] U.S. Energy Information Administration (EIA). 2020c. "Frequently Asked Questions (FAQs): How much gasoline does the United States consume?" Accessed October 27, 2020 at https://www.eia.gov/tools/faqs/faq.php?id=23&t=10#:~:text=In%202019%2C%20about%20142.71%20billion,9.31%20million%20barrels)%20per%20day.&text=There%20are%2042%20U.S.%20gallons%20in%20a%20barrel. Page last updated March 9, 2021.

[29] U.S. Energy Information Administration (EIA). 2020b. "U.S. energy facts explained." Accessed October 27, 2020 at https://www.eia.gov/energyexplained/us-energy-facts/.

[30] Ibid.

- Total energy (primary fuels plus electricity) by sector is: 28% transportation, 33% industry, 21% residential, and 18% commercial. Fossil fuel supplies nearly all of transportation energy needs.[31]

> - Worldwide, transportation breaks down approximately as follows: 50% cars/buses, 12% trucks, 13% marine, 10% air, 15% other (e.g., rail, pipelines).[32] Given the US love of cars and trucks and its global trade, the following is assumed for the US: 70% land, 15% marine, 12% air, and 3% other.

> - The electricity fraction of total energy used by each sector is: 74% commercial; 67% residential, 13% industrial, and transportation is negligible.[33]

- 37% of US primary fuels make electricity. Electricity is a "secondary" energy source because it is generated from primary fuels.[34]

---

[31] U.S. Energy Information Administration (EIA). 2021a. "Monthly Energy Review, March: Table 2.1 Energy Consumption by Sector." Accessed at https://www.eia.gov/totalenergy/data/monthly/pdf/sec2_3.pdf.

[32] The Maritime Executive. 2015. "Transport Uses 25 Percent of World Energy." November 19. Accessed October 27, 2020 at https://www.maritime-executive.com/article/transport-uses-25-percent-of-world-energy.

[33] U.S. Energy Information Administration (EIA). 2021a. "Monthly Energy Review, March: Table 2.1 Energy Consumption by Sector." Accessed at https://www.eia.gov/totalenergy/data/monthly/pdf/sec2_3.pdf.

[34] U.S. Energy Information Administration (EIA). 2021b. "Electricity consumption in the United States was about 3.8 trillion kilowatthours (kWh) in 2020." Accessed at https://www.eia.gov/energyexplained/electricity/use-of-electricity.php. Page last updated April 7, 2021.

- Electricity is generated from the following primary fuels: 38% natural gas, 24% coal, 20% nuclear, 18% renewables, and 0.5% petroleum.[35]

- There are currently 98 nuclear power plants in the US.

- US utility generation is about 4 trillion Kwh/yr. That is about 460 – 1Gw power plants (a typical modern plant size), if they ran at full capacity (they don't).

- A modern wind turbine has about a 2 MW capacity and can be expected to generate about 4 million Kwhr/yr.[36]

- A nuclear power plant costs about $10 billion for about 1 Gw capacity.[37]

- A 1 Gw power plant running at full capacity 24 hrs/day, 365 days/yr will generate 9 billion Kwh/yr.

---

[35] U.S. Energy Information Administration (EIA). 2021c. "What is U.S. electricity generation by energy source?" Accessed at https://www.eia.gov/tools/faqs/faq.php?id=427&t=3. Page last updated March 5, 2021.

[36] National Wind Watch. Undated. "FAQ -- Output." Accessed at https://www.wind-watch.org/faq-output.php#:~:text=What%20is%20the%20power%20capacity,range%20of%202%2D3%20MW.

[37] Schlissel, D & Biewald, B. 2008. "Nuclear Power Plant Construction Costs." Synapse Energy Economics, Inc., Cambridge, MA. 9p., July. Accessed at https://www.synapse-energy.com/sites/default/files/SynapsePaper.2008-07.0.Nuclear-Plant-Construction-Costs.A0022_0.pdf.

- A 12 Kw capacity solar array might be expected to generate about 12,000 Kwh/yr, depending on location.[38]

- 43% of residential energy use is for space heating/cooling (there are 110 million homes). [39] That is about 9 Quads. It is unclear how much residential space heating is electric HVAC. Assuming it is 20% would mean fossil residential space heating is 7.2 Quads, equivalent to generating 0.5 billion tons/yr of greenhouse gas.

- New home construction is around 1.4 million houses per year.[40]

- 25% of commercial energy use is for space heating/cooling. [41] That is 2.4 Quads, but again, the electric fraction is unknown. Assuming it is higher than residential, 50%, fossil-based commercial heating/cooling would be 1.2

---

[38] Energy Sage. 2021. "Solar panel cost in 2021: what price for solar can you expect?" Accessed at https://news.energysage.com/how-much-does-the-average-solar-panel-installation-cost-in-the-u-s/.

[39] Hamman, C. 2010. "Space Heating." Submitted as coursework for Physics 240, Stanford University, Fall 2010. Accessed at http://large.stanford.edu/courses/2010/ph240/hamman2/.

[40] U.S. Department of Commerce, U.S. Census Bureau. 2021. "Press Release: Monthly New Residential Construction, March 2021." Release No. CB21-61. April 16. Accessed at https://www.census.gov/construction/nrc/pdf/newresconst.pdf.

[41] SF Magazine. 2013. "Residential vs. Commercial Energy Use." March 21. Accessed at https://solarfeeds.com/residential-vs-commercial-energy-use/#:~:text=Commercial%20Energy%20Use%200&text=Combined%2C%20buildings%20in%20the%20United,consume%2040%25%20of%20all%20energy.&text=2)%20In%20terms%20of%20energy,energy%20as%20the%20commercial%20sector.

Quads, equivalent to about 0.1 billion tons/yr of greenhouse gas.

> - There are 6 million commercial buildings in the US with 90 billion sq ft of floor space.[42]

- The majority of industrial energy use is for "process heat." Assume that fossil-based space heating uses only about 5% of industrial energy (1.6 Quads, 0.1 billion tons/yr).

- Declining renewables costs, especially wind and solar, are making them competitive with traditional energy sources. Wind energy costs about $0.06/Kwh (3-12 cents range)[43] (the average US electric bill is at $0.12/Kwh); a 2 MW wind turbine (enough for 200 houses) costs about $4 million to install;[44] solar installation costs about $40,000 for 12 Kw of capacity[45] (enough for a typical house); Japan installed a large, 70 MW, solar array on 0.5 acres at a capital cost of

---

[42] Center for Sustainable Systems, University of Michigan. 2020b. "Commercial Buildings Factsheet." Pub. No. CSS05-05. Accessed at http://css.umich.edu/factsheets/commercial-buildings-factsheet#:~:text=In%20the%20U.S.%2C%205.6%20million,in%20floor%20space%20since%201979.&text=By%202050%2C%20commercial%20building%20floor,a%2034%25%20increase%20from%202019.

[43] International Renewable Energy Agency (IRENA). 2020. "Wind Power." Accessed at https://www.irena.org/costs/Power-Generation-Costs/Wind-Power.

[44] Windustry. "How Much Do Wind Turbines Cost?" 2016. Accessed at http://www.windustry.org/how_much_do_wind_turbines_cost#:~:text=The%20costs%20for%20a%20utility,%243%2D%244%20million%20installed.

[45] Energy Sage. 2021. "Solar panel cost in 2021: what price for solar can you expect?" Accessed at https://news.energysage.com/how-much-does-the-average-solar-panel-installation-cost-in-the-u-s/.

$44 million.[46] Geothermal heating is equivocal – expensive to install (about $30,000 per home), and expensive to run (electricity for pumps), but still perhaps 30% cheaper to run than burning fossil fuel. Biofuels are also equivocal – somewhat carbon neutral, but expensive to grow abundantly/quickly (e.g., algae and sugarcane) and to process into fuel.

- The US emitted 6.7 billion tons of carbon dioxide equivalents (greenhouse gases) in 2018.[47] According to the use sector breakdown above, this is 1.5 billion tons/yr from electricity generation (less renewables and nuclear), 1.9 billion tons/yr from transportation, 1.9 billion tons/yr from industry, 0.5 billion tons/yr from non-electric residential space heating, and perhaps 0.3 billion tons/yr from commercial (difficult to know how much is electric HVAC). Agriculture is about 20% of the total, about 0.6 billion tons/yr.

> - Renewables are not unscathed in this consideration. For example, decaying vegetation in hydropower reservoirs is a notorious greenhouse gas emitter.

---

[46] Kyocera. 2013. "KYOCERA Starts Operation of 70MW Solar Power Plant, the Largest in Japan." November 5. Accessed December 22, 2015, at: http://global.kyocera.com/news/2013/1101_nnms.html.

[47] U.S. Environmental Protection Agency (EPA). 2021. "Inventory of U.S. Greenhouse Gas Emissions and Sinks." Accessed at https://www.epa.gov/ghgemissions/inventory-us-greenhouse-gas-emissions-and-sinks. Last updated April 9, 2021.

- Carbon sequestration from the atmosphere currently costs about $600/ton with nascent technologies. Optimists in the field are hoping for $100/ton.[48]

Although these are useful facts, there are tricky overlaps, mainly because sectors use both primary fuels and electricity. Here are some manipulations of those US facts, sorting out the overlaps and complications:

Electricity – deducting renewables and nuclear, the remaining fossil-based generation totals 23 Quads (7 trillion Kwhr) and emits 1.5 billion tons/yr of greenhouse gas. (Remember, some additional greenhouse gas is also generated from renewables.)

Transportation – ground-based vehicles (cars, trucks, and buses) use 20 Quads and thus emit 1.3 billion tons/yr of greenhouse gas: air – 3.4 Quads, 0.23 billion tons/yr; marine – 4.2 Quads, 0.3 billion tons/yr; with about 0.6 Quad (0.01 billion tons/yr of greenhouse gas) remaining for things like railroads.

Space heating – Residential, commercial, and industry account for about 10 Quads and thus 0.7 billion tons/yr of greenhouse gas.

---

[48] Service, Robert F. 2018. "Cost plunges for capturing carbon dioxide from the air." June 7. Science. Accessed at https://www.sciencemag.org/news/2018/06/cost-plunges-capturing-carbon-dioxide-air.

Of the 2.6 billion tons/yr of greenhouse gas emissions remaining, about 1.5 billion tons/yr is from industrial processes, 0.7 is from agriculture, and the rest, 0.4, must be from all other sources and rounding.

This chapter shows what it will cost for the US to convert to sustainable, earth-friendly energy – a one-time cost of half of US GDP, plus ongoing costs at least equivalent to one-third of the US defense budget. Most of the required technology already exists, although more engineering for atmospheric carbon sequestration is needed, as are many infrastructure changes that will require more costs and have logistical issues. The bottom line, however, is that conversion is feasible. Let's get to work.

Sustainable Energy Plan Accounting

	Energy	Greenhouse Gas Emissions
Electric		
Current Fossil Use	23 Q*	1.54 Billon Tons-yr
Non-fossil	14 Q	0
Convert to Non-fossil	23Q = 7 TKwh**	-1.54
Remaining after 2040	37 TKwh non fossil	0
Transportation		
Current Fossil Use	28 Q	1.88
Non-fossil***	0	0
Convert to Non-fossil	20 Q = 6 TKwh	-1.34
Remaining after 2040	8 Q	0.54
Industrial		
Current Fossil Use	26.4 Q	1.77
Non-fossil	0	0
Convert to Non-fossil	13.2 Q = 4 TKwh	-0.88
Remaining after 2040	13.2 Q	0.88
Commercial		
Current Fossil Use	4.7 Q	0.31
Non-fossil	0	0
Convert to Non-fossil	1.1 Q = 0.3 TKwh	-0.1

Remaining after 2040	1.1 Q	0.21
Residential		
Current Fossil Use	7 Q	0.47
Non-fossil	0	0
Convert to Non-fossil	3.7 Q = 1.1 TKwh	-0.25
Remaining after 2040	3.7 Q	0.22
TOTAL New Electricity	17.1 TKwh	
TOTAL Remaining GH Gas		1.85 BTY

*   *Quadrillion BTU/yr (Quads). Note that 37Q of electricity is generated but there are system losses.*

*** Trillion Kilowatt hours/yr*

**** "Non-fossil" means within the sector and does not mean any non-fossil component in electricity used.*

5   Other Issues

The issues noted in the preceding chapters are not the only ones facing those living in America. A few of the other issues with some simplified considerations are as follows:

<u>Product Safety</u>. A major share of health risks threatening most people is from chemicals in the products in their home, such as cleaning and personal care products. The exposures from these products, which you rub on your skin and which vaporize into the air you breathe, are real. Labelling regulations require the products to list the "active" ingredients, i.e., those doing the job claimed by the product, while lumping everything else under the heading, "inactive ingredients." But many of those "inactive" ingredients are far from inactive from a health perspective. In fact, some of them are carcinogens. But you will never know that until products are labelled for their safety. Such labeling could involve something similar to the energy "five-star" system with a bar code on the label for more information, summoned via your smartphone. Then you could make a buying decision based not just on efficacy but also on safety.

<u>Your Data</u>. Not only is the government monitoring every call, click, and movement (Snowden is right), but the internet companies are accumulating and using data that you <u>give</u> them about yourself for increasingly more manipulative purposes. You willingly, or unknowingly, give it to them in return for them giving you their wares for free. It would be better for you to choose to opt into data-gathering, as in opt in – free, or opt out – pay for the service. Maybe there's some middle ground, depending how much of their "Agree to

Terms" you're willing to agree to. Most apps/software won't let you download/proceed *at all* unless you agree to give up all your rights and data in fine print that few ever read. You should have a choice as to what terms you agree to and let the vendor decide if they still want you as a user. All of this would require new business models on the providers' part, but so what? That's their business.

The Electoral College. Get rid of it. It is an outdated concept that doesn't align with most people's view of what American democracy is – representative voting. The Electoral College was devised at a time when state's rights were much more emphasized over a federal government than is currently the case. In addition, the Founders still had a bit of feudalistic elitism in them, and feared that rule by the mob (i.e., the popular vote) was to be avoided. During modern presidential elections, people become confused when a candidate can win the popular vote but lose the election. That is because they believe in representative voting but are getting something different.

The Supreme Court. Under the US system of advice and consent, it is the Senate that approves new Supreme Court justices. Yet, similar to the Electoral College issues of poor representation, this means that Supreme Court justices can be approved by a Senate majority that represents as little as 18% of the US population. This can politicize the one arm of government that is not supposed to be political. Fix it. Also, change appointments to 16 years rather than life, so new blood keeps rotating in and each president gets two appointments.

College. Part of the American dream has been for the next generation to be better educated than the last. This often translated to almost automatically going to college, whereas your parents didn't. But 40% of college grads never use/need their degree, and only 60% of jobs require a college degree or partial, similar training (e.g., community college). Student debt currently totals $1.6 trillion. Many young people have college debts in the tens or hundreds of thousands of dollars, which will not be paid off until they are in late middle age. This affects the economy and their lives. As an alternative to college, young people should consider the trades. The trades can offer lucrative careers, are challenging, and they are critically short of workers. US society tends to demean such career paths, whereas other societies, such as Germany, honor them. Not only is this an opportunity for high school grads, but it is a necessity for society to function. The need for a pathway through college for all should be reexamined.

Incarceration. There are about 2.2 million people in US prisons, 60% of whom are there for drugs. Some portion of that 60% is hardcore, e.g., kingpins, and they should stay there, but a large portion are people for whom prison is worse than rehabilitation. We should find a better way to deal with them.

Infrastructure. The American Society of Civil Engineers gives the current state of America's infrastructure a grade of D+, and estimates it would take $3.6 trillion to make it right.[49] Our infrastructure is bad and getting worse, even unsafe. One in nine bridges is structurally deficient; we've already seen a few collapse. Schools are getting so

---

[49] American Society of Civil Engineers (ASCE). 2021. "Report Card for America's Infrastructure." Accessed at http://www.infrastructurereportcard.org/.

poorly funded that Chicago teachers and Boston students have recently taken to the streets. Our 100-year-old water supply infrastructure is nearing the end of its useful life, as shown by the 250,000 water main breaks every year. Why is this important issue being ignored? One answer is that its timeframe is beyond that of most politicians. Why should they take the hit for spending money that won't bring benefits until after they are gone? The lack of political will about infrastructure is shameful. America seems to have lost its vision and willingness to create a future for itself. We believe we are already there. Gone are the days when we knuckled down and built. During the Depression we put a CCC (civilian conservation corps) to work building infrastructure rather than just sitting around. Now, we wait for a crisis to deal with almost everything. Infrastructure just may become a crisis; will we be able to deal if it does? Perhaps, but wouldn't visionary leadership and political guts today be better to avoid those bumps in the road tomorrow?

Immigration. Immigration has been essential throughout US history, yet Americans tend to dislike immigrants and pass laws to prove it. For example, of the more than 40 immigration laws passed since the 1700s, some of the most egregious were the 1882 Chinese Exclusion Act, the 1921 Emergency Quota Act, and the 1954 Operation Wetback. Current US law/policy allows for 675,000 permanent immigrant visas per year with, theoretically, no limit on the number of US citizen spouses, children, or parents also allowed. In practice, however, there are caps on this at around 450,000/yr. Permanent employment-based immigration is limited to 140,000/yr and there are 20 different types of temporary employment visas. Within the former category is the "Einstein Visa," Melania Trump's entrance ticket, which according to the law is reserved for 40,000 "[P]ersons of extraordinary ability" in the arts, science, education, business, or athletics, and outstanding professors, researchers, multinational executives, and managers. Immigration from any one country cannot exceed 7% of the total US immigration per year. Refugees with legitimate fear of persecution or for their safety are also admitted to the US with the president annually defining groups in this category, and caps for regions of the world. They must apply from outside of the US to be considered a refugee, and there are rules defining what constitutes a legitimate reason. Having been as high as 110,000 in 2017[50], the world cap for 2020 is set at 18,000. Asylum seekers (must apply from inside the US) have no cap, with the same refugee rules for acceptance. Each year, 55,000 Diversity Visas are granted for immigration from countries having previously low rates of immigration. Temporary Protected Status (TPS) is granted to people who are in the US but cannot return to their home country because of a "natural disaster," "extraordinary temporary conditions," or "ongoing armed conflict." TPS is granted to a country for 6, 12, or 18 months and can be extended beyond that if unsafe conditions in the country persist. TPS does not necessarily lead to "Green Card" status (the credential required for naturalization, obtainable via a US citizen family member or employer petition), nor does it confer any other immigration status. Finally, there are 700,000 people (formerly under 16

---

[50] Mhajne, A & Whetstone, C. 2021. "The United States Can't Welcome More Refugees Without Reforming Its Resettlement System." Foreign Policy (FP). April 12. Accessed April 24, 2021 at https://foreignpolicy.com/2021/04/12/trump-gutted-refugee-resettlement-biden-reform/.

who are in the US not necessarily due to their choice, e.g., as children of undocumented people) in the US who are temporarily protected under DACA (Deferred Action for Childhood Arrivals). In order to qualify for US citizenship through naturalization, an individual must have had a Green Card for at least five years (or three years if he or she obtained the green card through a US-citizen spouse or through the Violence Against Women Act, VAWA).

Most economists will agree that immigration is critical to maintaining a country's economy. Throughout our history, immigrants have taken the necessary jobs that more longstanding Americans didn't want to, from building the railroads and other infrastructure to agriculture and maintenance. Such needs continue to exist in the US. Some of the current immigration debate has become heated about the system being abused, but actually, many immigration problems arise *due to lack of enforcement of existing laws*. Most Americans want fair and compassionate immigration laws/policies that are enforced; few, if any, want "open borders." If current laws were enforced, we would probably go a long way to solving immigration problems. We should consider new technologies to help with this enforcement. And we should resolve our current immigration transgressions (i.e., the DACA people and the 11 million "illegal aliens"). Make DACA people totally legal (it was not their doing). Give the 11 million a "special status," defined as: legal residency, paying taxes, but not allowed to vote. If all of that is not enough, we must first ask, "what immigration policy do we actually want and need?"

Guns. The gun situation in the US today, with its mass shooting violence and assault weapon "rights," has gone well beyond what the Founders imagined for the Second Amendment. In those days before a US Army, King George had left us with a wariness of possible government tyranny and arming citizen militias was a matter of national defense. Today, the NRA (National Rifle Association) gives $2 million to high school shooting clubs, there are more guns in America than people, and US gun violence is 50 times that of the UK, 60 times China, and 100 times Japan. Our children are being slaughtered; 77% of the population wants better gun control, but our politicians do nothing, or worse, go backwards. In 2016, the NRA spent $58 million buying politicians for gun insanity: $1 million of direct political contributions, $3 million for lobbying, and $54 million of dark money [Political action committees (PACs), 501c, etc., thanks to the Supreme Court's *Citizens United* decision]. This is actually a small amount if you think about it. It shows how cheaply our politicians can be bought (a typical NRA campaign contribution is $10,000).

The NRA and its political lackeys have a new argument against gun control – it's not a gun problem, it's a mental health problem. Of course people who kill people have a mental health problem. But they would kill less without guns. The US gun issue will not be solved until the NRA gets out of politics and until the Second Amendment can be viewed outside of originalist constitutional thinking.

<u>Made In America</u>. Even American flags are made in China. The US has lost 5 million manufacturing jobs over the last 20 years. The irony is that our consumers' demand for cheap goods is putting them out of work. What is the best balance of offshore/onshore supply for the US? The COVID-19 pandemic in 2020 demonstrated some advantages to shorter, onshore supply chains, but where should we draw the line to optimize creative growth while minimizing commoditized drudgery? For years our excuse was that we didn't need to be an industrial economy because we were a growing service economy. Now even the service jobs are outsourced. This is a complex issue, but its basic solution is not with tariffs and trade wars. Instead, the problems will be fixed with good old competitiveness. Like it or not, the US lives in a global economy and our success in it will not be coercion and nostalgia, it will be innovation and quality.

<u>Elections and Campaigns</u>. The 2020 Presidential campaigns spent almost $7 billion. Some Senate races recently crossed the $200 million mark. President Trump started campaigning for 2020 almost as soon as he was seated in 2017, spending about $3 million of taxpayer money every time he took Airforce One to political campaign rallies, not to mention distractions from his real job. Besides the offensive sums, a growing problem with large campaign financing is that the increasing funds must come from outside the states of a given campaign. This makes local politics no longer local. Enabled by the Supreme Court's 2010 Citizens United decision that permits the formation of PACs and SuperPACs, the trend is for nationwide party forces to shape Congress by funding money into local campaigns that can tilt party dominance. This distorts true state representation. Presidential abuse of the office to achieve political gain argues against allowing for more than one term. Let's try only one presidential term of six years with no reelection opportunity. This would allow longer time for achieving an agenda with no distractions. Revoke Citizens United and impose campaign spending limits and let's see if we can keep elections local with messages that contain better quality over quantity. Substantial money could be saved by using modern technology for campaigning. This means websites with substantive information on issue positions, rather than millions of advertisements and campaign speeches filled with blathering and dubious attacks.

www.ingramcontent.com/pod-product-compliance
Lightning Source LLC
Chambersburg PA
CBHW061524250726
48657CB00005B/2055